GETTING TO KNOW YOUR LOWER NATURE

OTHER BOOKS BY SUSAN GAMMAGE

GETTING TO KNOW YOUR LOWER NATURE

A BAHÁ'Í PERSPECTIVE

Susan Gammage

Nine Star Solutions, Publisher

Muskoka

www.ninestarsolutions.com

ISBN: 978-0-9936776-5-6

DEDICATION

For Vera and Peter

And for

Val and Karl

And for

Michael and Sarah

And for

Chris

And With Profound Gratitude to the Divine Physician

TABLE OF CONTENTS

THE DUAL NATURE OF MAN

What We Know About Our Dual Nature

In man there are two expressions, one is the expression of nature, the other the expression of the spiritual realm:

> In man there are two expressions, one is the expression of nature, the other the expression of the spiritual realm. ('Abdu'l-Bahá, Foundations of World Unity, p. 77)

Every good habit or noble quality belongs to man's spiritual nature, whereas all his imperfections and sinful actions are born of his material nature.

> Every good habit, every noble quality belongs to man's spiritual nature, whereas all his imperfections and sinful actions are born of his material nature. ('Abdu'l-Bahá, Paris Talks, p. 60)

In the lower nature, we live for the world alone; in the higher, we approach God.

> In one he approaches God, in the other he lives for the world alone. ('Abdu'l-Bahá, Paris Talks, p. 60)

In our material nature man expresses untruth, cruelty and injustice; whereas in his Divine nature we find love, mercy, kindness, truth and justice.

> In his material aspect he expresses untruth, cruelty
> and injustice; all these are the outcome of his
> lower nature. The attributes of his Divine nature
> are shown forth in love, mercy, kindness, truth
> and justice, one and all being expressions of his
> higher nature. ('Abdu'l-Bahá, Paris Talks, p. 60)

Isn't it strange that man, despite being created with an
ideal power and a conscious spirit, will descend to a level
beneath him where he considers matter the ruler of his
existence and denies that which lies beyond? In this sense,
he's no better than the animal.

> How strange then it seems that man,
> notwithstanding his endowment with this ideal
> power, will descend to a level beneath him and
> declare himself no greater than that which is
> manifestly inferior to his real station. God has
> created such a conscious spirit within him that he
> is the most wonderful of all contingent beings. In
> ignoring these virtues he descends to the material
> plane, considers matter the ruler of existence and
> denies that which lies beyond. Is this virtue? In its
> fullest sense this is animalistic, for the animal
> realizes nothing more. (Abdu'l-Baha, The
> Promulgation of Universal Peace, p. 178-179)

All the imperfections found in the animal are found in
man (antagonism, hatred and selfish struggle for
existence; jealousy, revenge, ferocity, cunning, hypocrisy,
greed, injustice and tyranny). On the other hand, we also
find in him justice, sincerity, faithfulness, knowledge,
wisdom, illumination, mercy and pity coupled with
intellect, comprehension, the power to grasp the realities

of things and the ability to penetrate the truths of existence.

> All the imperfections found in the animal are found in man. In him there is antagonism, hatred and selfish struggle for existence; in his nature lurk jealousy, revenge, ferocity, cunning, hypocrisy, greed, injustice and tyranny. So to speak, the reality of man is clad in the outer garment of the animal, the habiliments of the world of nature, the world of darkness, imperfections and unlimited baseness.

> On the other hand, we find in him justice, sincerity, faithfulness, knowledge, wisdom, illumination, mercy and pity coupled with intellect, comprehension, the power to grasp the realities of things and the ability to penetrate the truths of existence. All these great perfections are to be found in man . . . The animal nature is darkness; the heavenly is light in light. (Abdu'l-Baha, Foundations of World Unity, p. 110)

Although man shares many qualities with the animal, particularly at the level of the lower nature, it is evident that man is more noble and superior. In man there is an ideal power surpassing nature. He has consciousness, volition, memory, intelligent power, divine attributes and virtues of which nature is completely deprived. Man is higher and nobler because of the heavenly forces latent and manifest in him.

> Altogether it is evident that man is more noble and superior; that in him there is an ideal power surpassing nature. He has consciousness, volition,

> memory, intelligent power, divine attributes and virtues of which nature is completely deprived, bereft and minus; therefore man is higher and nobler by reason of the ideal and heavenly force latent and manifest in him. ('Abdu'l-Baha, Foundations of World Unity, p. 70)

Man is instinctively and consciously intelligent; fortified with memory and able to discover the mysteries of nature. As an animal man is subject to nature, but in his spiritual or conscious being he transcends the world of material existence. His spiritual powers possess virtues which enable him to triumph over natural conditions. These ideal virtues or powers in man enable him to comprehend natural laws and phenomena, penetrate the mysteries of the unknown and invisible and bring them forth into the realm of the known and visible.

> Man is intelligent, instinctively and consciously intelligent; nature is not. Man is fortified with memory; nature does not possess it. Man is the discoverer of the mysteries of nature; nature is not conscious of those mysteries herself. It is evident, therefore, that man is dual in aspect: as an animal he is subject to nature, but in his spiritual or conscious being he transcends the world of material existence. His spiritual powers, being nobler and higher, possess virtues of which nature intrinsically has no evidence; therefore, they triumph over natural conditions. These ideal virtues or powers in man surpass or surround nature, comprehend natural laws and phenomena, penetrate the mysteries of the unknown and invisible and bring them forth into the realm of the known and visible. ('Abdu'l-Bahá, The Promulgation of Universal Peace, p. 80-81)

Our higher nature brings forth patience, longing desire, true understanding and love. The lower breeds arrogance, vainglory and conceit. It's only result is iniquity and rebellion; and it bears no fruit but the poison of hatred and envy under a shadow of consuming fire.

> Know verily that Knowledge is of two kinds: Divine and Satanic. The one welleth out from the fountain of divine inspiration; the other is but a reflection of vain and obscure thoughts. The source of the former is God Himself; the motive-force of the latter the whisperings of selfish desire. The one is guided by the principle: "Fear ye God; God will teach you;" the other is but a confirmation of the truth: "Knowledge is the most grievous veil between man and his Creator. The former bringeth forth the fruit of patience, of longing desire, of true understanding, and love; whilst the latter can yield naught but arrogance, vainglory and conceit. From the sayings of those Masters of holy utterance, Who have expounded the meaning of true knowledge, the odour of these dark teachings, which have obscured the world, can in no wise be detected. The tree of such teachings can yield no result except iniquity and rebellion, and beareth no fruit but hatred and envy. Its fruit is deadly poison; its shadow a consuming fire. (Baha'u'llah, The Kitab-i-Iqan, p. 68)

None of us spend our lives entirely in one world or another – our reality stands between the two natures:

> As we have before indicated, this human reality
> stands between the higher and the lower in man,
> between the world of the animal and the world of
> divinity. (Abdu'l-Baha, Foundations of World
> Unity, p. 110)

Or even three (animal, human and divine):

> Therefore we say that man is a reality which
> stands between light and darkness. From this
> standpoint of view, his nature is threefold, animal,
> human and divine. (Abdu'l-Baha, Foundations of
> World Unity, p. 110)

If man's animal side becomes predominant, he becomes
lower than the brute, whereas if his heavenly powers
become predominant, he becomes the most superior being
in the world of existence. 'Abdu'l-Bahá is reported to have
said:

> This human reality stands between two grades,
> between the world of the animal and the world of
> Divinity. Were the animal in man to become
> predominant, man would become even lower than
> the brute. Were the heavenly powers in man to
> become predominant, man would become the
> most superior being in the world of existence.
> ('Abdu'l-Baha, Star of the West, vol. VII, no. 8,
> August 1, 1916)

We all have the ability to choose good or evil. If our
power for good predominates and our inclination to do
wrong is conquered, we can be called saints.

> If a man's Divine nature dominates his human
> nature, we have a saint. Man has the power both
> to do good and to do evil; if his power for good
> predominates and his inclinations to do wrong are
> conquered, then man in truth may be called a
> saint. But if, on the contrary, he rejects the things
> of God and allows his evil passions to conquer
> him, then he is no better than a mere animal.
> ('Abdu'l-Bahá, Paris Talks, p. 60)

The choice is up to us.

Everyone's life has both a dark and bright side. The key is
to turn our backs to the darkness and our faces to 'Abdu'l-
Bahá.

> Everyone's life has both a dark and bright side.
> The Master said: turn your back to the darkness
> and your face to Me. (Shoghi Effendi, The
> Unfolding Destiny of the British Bahá'í
> Community, p. 457)

Why do we have a dual nature?

We seem to need contrasts. If there was no wrong, how
would we recognize the right? If there was no sin, how
would we appreciate virtue? If evil deeds were unknown
how could you commend good actions? If sickness did not
exist how would you understand health?

> If there was no wrong how would you recognize
> the right? If it were not for sin how would you
> appreciate virtue? If evil deeds were unknown
> how could you commend good actions? If sickness
> did not exist how would you understand health?

('Abdu'l-Bahá, Foundations of World Unity, p. 76-79)

How do we tell the difference between inspiration from the lower nature or higher?

Knowledge is of two kinds: Divine and Satanic. The one comes from the fountain of divine inspiration; the other is a reflection of vain and obscure thoughts. The source of the former is God Himself; the motive of the latter comes from the whisperings of selfish desire.

> Know verily that Knowledge is of two kinds: Divine and Satanic. The one welleth out from the fountain of divine inspiration; the other is but a reflection of vain and obscure thoughts. The source of the former is God Himself; the motive-force of the latter the whisperings of selfish desire. The one is guided by the principle: "Fear ye God; God will teach you;" the other is but a confirmation of the truth: "Knowledge is the most grievous veil between man and his Creator." (Baha'u'llah, The Kitab-i-Iqan, p. 68)

How can we tell if an inspiration comes from God or our lower nature, when both are the influx of the human heart?

> What is inspiration? It is the influx of the human heart. But what are satanic promptings which afflict mankind? They are the influx of the heart also. How shall we differentiate between them? ('Abdu'l-Bahá, The Promulgation of Universal Peace, p. 22)

It's simple! Every good thing is of God, and every evil thing is from us.

> Every good thing is of God, and every evil thing is from yourselves. Will ye not comprehend? (Bahá'u'lláh, Gleanings from the Writings of Bahá'u'lláh, p. 149)

We can have conversations with our higher selves:

> As in a dream one talks with a friend while the mouth is silent, so is it in the conversation of the spirit. A man may converse with the ego within him saying: "May I do this? Would it be advisable for me to do this work?" Such as this is conversation with the higher self. ('Abdu'l-Bahá, Paris Talks, p. 178)

Summary

So to summarize the difference between the animal (and lower part of ourselves); and our higher selves:

Animal Nature	Higher Nature
Inert	Progressive
Unconscious	Conscious
No volition and acts	Mighty will
Not in touch with the realm of God	Attuned to evidences of the realm of God
Uninformed of God	Conscious of God

Denied of virtues	Acquires Divine virtues
No power to modify the influence of its instincts	can voluntarily discontinue vices
No intelligence	Instinctively and consciously intelligent
Unconscious of the mysteries of nature	Able to discover the mysteries of nature
Subject to nature	Able to transcend the material nature
Unable to comprehend natural laws	Comprehends natural laws and phenomena
Hidden secrets remain latent and concealed	Able to penetrate the mysteries of the unknown and invisible and bring them forth into the realm of the known and visible.
Unable to create	Creates all the existing arts and sciences
antagonism, hatred and selfish struggle for existence	justice, sincerity, faithfulness, knowledge, wisdom, illumination, mercy and pity
jealousy, revenge, ferocity, cunning, hypocrisy, greed, injustice and tyranny	intellect, comprehension, the power to grasp the realities of things and the ability to penetrate the truths of

	existence
untruth, cruelty and injustice	love, mercy, kindness, truth and justice

In addition, man is more noble and superior to the animal because in him is an ideal power which includes his consciousness, volition, memory, intelligent power, divine attributes and virtues.

WHAT WE KNOW ABOUT OUR LOWER NATURE

What is Our Lower Nature?

Anything that is contrary to the will of God comes from our lower nature, or ego.

> This would be contrary to the will of God and according to the will of Satan, by which we mean the natural inclinations of the lower nature. ('Abdu'l-Bahá, The Promulgation of Universal Peace, p. 286-287)

Whatever is interpreted as evil refers to the lower nature in man.

> The evil spirit, Satan or whatever is interpreted as evil, refers to the lower nature in man. ('Abdu'l-Bahá, Foundations of World Unity, p. 76-79)

Our baser nature is symbolized in various ways:

> This baser nature is symbolized in various ways. ('Abdu'l-Bahá, Foundations of World Unity, p. 76-79)

Often, it's symbolized as Satan, described as the evil ego within us rather than an evil personality outside.

This lower nature in man is symbolized as Satan —
the evil ego within us, not an evil personality
outside. ('Abdu'l-Bahá, The Promulgation of
Universal Peace, p. 286-287)

God never created an evil spirit – these ideas have always
been symbols of our earthly nature:

God has never created an evil spirit; all such ideas
and nomenclature are symbols expressing the
mere human or earthly nature of man. ('Abdu'l-
Bahá, Foundations of World Unity, p. 76-79)

The greatest of degradations is to leave the Shadow of God
and enter under the shadow of Satan (or our ego or lower
nature).

The greatest of degradation is to leave the Shadow
of God and enter under the shadow of Satan.
('Abdu'l-Bahá, Star of the West, Vol. 13, No. 1,
March 21, pp. 19-25)

Characteristics of the Lower Nature

All the imperfections found in animals are also found in
man. Innate in man is rancour; the struggle for existence;
the propensity for warfare; love of self; jealousy;
hypocrisy, slyness, greed, ignorance, injustice, tyranny
and so on. Our reality, therefore, is clad in the garment of
the animal or the world of nature. It's a world of
darkness; imperfection, and infinite baseness.

For instance, consider in man there is rancor, in
man there is struggle for existence; in the nature of
man there is propensity for warfare; innate in man

there is love of self; in him there is jealousy, and so
on with all the other imperfections and thus, in a
word, all the imperfections found in the animal
are to be found in man. For instance, in the animal
there is ferocity; there is also ferocity in man. In
the animal there is what is called hypocrisy or
slyness, like unto that in the fox; and in the animal
there is greed -- and there is ignorance. So there
are all these in man. In the animal there are
injustice and tyranny; so likewise are they in man.
The reality of man, therefore, is clad, you might
say, in its outer form in the garment of the animal,
in the garment of the world of nature, of the world
of darkness; that is the world of imperfection, that
is the world of infinite baseness. ('Abdu'l-Baha,
Star of the West, vol. VII, no. 8, August 1, 1916)

Whenever you see jealousy, greed, the struggle for
survival, deception, hypocrisy, tyranny, oppression,
disputes, strife, bloodshed, looting and pillaging, which all
emanate from the world of nature, you realize that we are
all immersed in the world of nature to one degree or
another.

Today all people are immersed in the world of
nature. That is why thou dost see jealousy, greed,
the struggle for survival, deception, hypocrisy,
tyranny, oppression, disputes, strife, bloodshed,
looting and pillaging, which all emanate from the
world of nature. ('Abdu'l-Bahá, Selections from
the Writings of 'Abdu'l-Bahá, p. 206)

Sins such as injustice, tyranny, hatred, hostility and strife
are characteristics of the lower nature:

Sin is the state of man in the world of the baser nature, for in nature exist defects such as injustice, tyranny, hatred, hostility, strife: these are characteristics of the lower plane of nature. These are the sins of the world, the fruits of the tree from which Adam did eat. (Abdu'l-Baha, Paris Talks, p. 177)

The lower nature appeals to everyone differently, according to each person's own way:

Satan appears in different robes and appeals to everyone according to each person's own way. ('Abdu'l-Bahá, Star of the West, Vol. 13, No. 1, March 21, pp. 19-25)

The lower nature can be manipulated by others:

A strong-willed man, by appealing to the lower nature of man, or exciting the people's sentiments, may succeed in bringing about an uprising or a revolution in which he himself becomes the focal point. (Adib Taherzadeh, The Revelation of Bahá'u'lláh v 2, p. 123)

How?

Other people will try to mislead you through temptations which arouse the desires of self and cause you to follow your own lower nature, taking you away from God.

It is clear to your honor that before long Satan, in the garb of man, will reach that land and will try to mislead the friends of the Divine Beauty through temptations which arouse the desires of

self, and will cause them to follow the footsteps of
Satan away from the right and glorious path, and
prevent them from attaining the Blessed Shore of
the King of Oneness. This is a hidden information
of which we have informed the chosen ones lest
they may be deprived of their praiseworthy
station by associating with the embodiments of
hatred. ('Abdu'l-Bahá, Star of the West, Vol. 13,
No. 1, March 21, pp. 19-25)

We need to do everything we can to protect ourselves,
because if our lower nature has its way, we will be stuck in
it, with no promptings from our higher nature to help us
get free:

Endeavor to your utmost to protect yourselves,
because Satan appears in different robes and
appeals to everyone according to each person's
own way, until he becomes like unto him—then
he will leave him alone. ('Abdu'l-Bahá, Star of the
West, Vol. 13, No. 1, March 21, pp. 19-25)

Why do we have a lower nature?

We seem to need opposites in life. In this case, we see that
even the world of nature is defective:

The world of nature is defective. Look at it clearly,
casting aside all superstition and imagination . . .
It is an essential condition of the soil of earth that
thorns, weeds and fruitless trees may grow from
it. Relatively speaking, this is evil; it is simply the
lower state and baser product of nature. ('Abdu'l-
Bahá, Foundations of World Unity, p. 77)

The struggle between our lower nature and the Divine
teachings draw us towards our true station.

> The struggle between the forces of darkness —
> man's lower nature — and the rising sun of the
> Divine teachings which draw him on to his true
> station, intensifies day by day. (The Universal
> House of Justice, Messages 1963 to 1986, p. 113)

Effects of Living in our Lower Nature

When we are captives of our self and desire, engulfed in
the passions of our lower nature, we find wealth and fame
and enjoy the comforts of life, but in the end, the outcome
is always utter evanescence and oblivion. No trace of us
remains; no fruit; no result; no benefit to carry forward to
eternity.

> Consider the human world. See how nations have
> come and gone. They have been of all minds and
> purposes. Some were mere captives of self and
> desire, engulfed in the passions of the lower
> nature. They attained to wealth, to the comforts of
> life, to fame. And what was the final outcome?
> Utter evanescence and oblivion. Reflect upon this.
> Look upon it with the eye of admonition. No trace
> of them remains, no fruit, no result, no benefit;
> they have gone utterly — complete effacement.
> ('Abdu'l-Bahá, The Promulgation of Universal
> Peace, p. 186)

When we follow the promptings of the self, it takes us
insistently to wickedness and lust.

> Follow not the promptings of the self, for it
> summoneth insistently to wickedness and lust.
> (Bahá'u'lláh, The Kitáb-i-Aqdas, p. 41)

The desires of our lower nature have altered the face of creation.

> Fear God, and follow not your desires which have altered the face of creation. (Bahá'u'lláh, The Proclamation of Bahá'u'lláh, p. 75)

If the spiritual qualities of the soul are never used, they become atrophied, enfeebled, and at last incapable. Unhappy and misguided, we become more savage; more unjust; more vile; more cruel and more malevolent than the lower animals themselves. When all our aspirations and desires are being strengthened by the lower side of our soul's nature, we become more and more brutal, until our whole being is worse than the beasts that perish.

> But on the other hand, when man does not open his mind and heart to the blessing of the spirit, but turns his soul towards the material side, towards the bodily part of his nature, then is he fallen from his high place and he becomes inferior to the inhabitants of the lower animal kingdom. In this case the man is in a sorry plight! For if the spiritual qualities of the soul, open to the breath of the Divine Spirit, are never used, they become atrophied, enfeebled, and at last incapable; whilst the soul's material qualities alone being exercised, they become terribly powerful—and the unhappy, misguided man, becomes more savage, more unjust, more vile, more cruel, more malevolent than the lower animals themselves. All his aspirations and desires being strengthened by the lower side of the soul's nature, he becomes more and more brutal, until his whole being is in no way superior to that of the beasts that perish. ('Abdu'l-Bahá, Paris Talks, p. 97)

Our lower nature and those of the people around us are
dangerous because, by standing as "observation posts",
they prevent us from taking the path to God, by every
means of deception and ruse possible:

> . . . the manifestations of Satan are occupying
> today the observation posts of the glorious path of
> God, and preventing the people by every means of
> deception and ruse. Before long you will witness
> the turning away of the people of Bayan from the
> Manifestation of the Merciful. ('Abdu'l-Bahá, Star
> of the West, Vol. 13, No. 1, March 21, pp. 19-25)

'Abdu'l-Bahá compares those who chose to stay in their
lower natures to the earthworm, whose highest aim is to
struggle to dig down to the depths of the earth despite the
fact that they are bound by a thousand cares and sorrows;
never safe from danger, or secure from sudden death.
After a brief span, they are utterly effaced, and no sign
remains to tell of them, and no word of them is ever heard
again.

> But the pitiable earthworms love only to tunnel
> into the ground, and what a mighty struggle they
> make to get themselves down into its depths!
> Even so are the sons of earth. Their highest aim is
> to augment their means of continuing on, in this
> vanishing world, this death in life; and this despite
> the fact that they are bound hand and foot by a
> thousand cares and sorrows, and never safe from
> danger, not even for the twinkling of an eye; never
> at any time secure, even from sudden death.
> Wherefore, after a brief span, are they utterly
> effaced, and no sign remaineth to tell of them, and
> no word of them is ever heard again. ('Abdu'l-

> Bahá, Selections from the Writings of 'Abdu'l-
> Bahá, p. 175-176)

Is this really the life we want to live?

How do we stay trapped in our lower nature?

Since we were created noble; in the image of God; a mine
rich in gems of inestimable value, what causes us to
change?

We stop paying attention to the Kingdom of God, and step
off His path. We remain attached to worldly attractions.
We've become defiled with qualities which are not
praiseworthy in the sight of God. We have become so
completely steeped in material issues and tendencies that
we fail to partake of the virtues of humanity.

> We have forsaken the path of God; we have given
> up attention to the divine Kingdom; we have not
> severed the heart from worldly attractions; we
> have become defiled with qualities which are not
> praiseworthy in the sight of God; we are so
> completely steeped in material issues and
> tendencies that we are not partakers of the virtues
> of humanity. ('Abdu'l-Bahá, The Promulgation of
> Universal Peace, p. 186)

Breaking Free

'Abdu'l-Bahá tells us that man can become conscious;
discover the mysteries and realities of life; be in touch with
the realm of God; use his mighty will to rule over his
lower nature; modify the influence of his instincts;
voluntarily discontinue vices; acquire divine virtues and
make progress:

It is evident, therefore, that man is ruler over nature's sphere and province. Nature is inert; man is progressive. Nature has no consciousness; man is endowed with it. Nature is without volition and acts perforce, whereas man possesses a mighty will. Nature is incapable of discovering mysteries or realities, whereas man is especially fitted to do so. Nature is not in touch with the realm of God; man is attuned to its evidences. Nature is uninformed of God; man is conscious of Him. Man acquires divine virtues; nature is denied them. Man can voluntarily discontinue vices; nature has no power to modify the influence of its instincts. ('Abdu'l-Baha, Promulgation of Universal Peace, p. 177-178)

He can't do it by himself, though. The soul needs training and guidance to get beyond the lower nature:

Briefly; the journey of the soul is necessary. The pathway of life is the road which leads to divine knowledge and attainment. Without training and guidance the soul could never progress beyond the conditions of its lower nature which is ignorant and defective. ('Abdu'l-Bahá, Foundations of World Unity, p. 76-79)

Man's outlook on life is too crude and materialistic to enable us to elevate ourselves into the higher realms of the spirit, so religion's role is to improve and transform us.

Man's outlook on life is too crude and materialistic to enable him to elevate himself into the higher realms of the spirit. It is this condition, so sadly morbid, into which society has fallen, that religion

seeks to improve and transform. (Shoghi Effendi,
Lights of Guidance, p. 134)

The Manifestations of God come into the world to dispel
the darkness of our animal nature and purify us from our
imperfections so that our spiritual nature can become
quickened, our divine qualities awakened, our perfections
made visible, our potential powers revealed and all the
virtues of the world of humanity latent within us to come
to life.

They are the educators, trainers and teachers able to
liberate us from the darkness of our lower nature, deliver
us from despair, error, ignorance, imperfections and all
evil qualities.

They clothe us in the garment of perfections and virtues;
make us wise and lead us into kingdoms of light and love.
They cause us to become just; sever us from self and
desire; make us meek, humble and friendly. They make
us heavenly; transform us and develop us into maturity.
They endow us with wealth and uplift us into dignity,
nobility and loftiness.

> The holy Manifestations of God come into the
> world to dispel the darkness of the animal or
> physical nature of man, to purify him from his
> imperfections in order that his heavenly and
> spiritual nature may become quickened, his divine
> qualities awakened, his perfections visible, his
> potential powers revealed and all the virtues of
> the world of humanity latent within him may
> come to life. These holy Manifestations of God are
> the educators and trainers of the world of
> existence, the teachers of the world of humanity.

> They liberate man from the darkness of the world
> of nature, deliver him from despair, error,
> ignorance, imperfections and all evil qualities.
> They clothe him in the garment of perfections and
> exalted virtues. Men are ignorant; the
> Manifestations of God make them wise. They are
> animalistic; the Manifestations make them human.
> They are savage and cruel; the Manifestations lead
> them into kingdoms of light and love. They are
> unjust; the Manifestations cause them to become
> just. Man is selfish; they sever him from self and
> desire. Man is haughty; they make him meek,
> humble and friendly. He is earthly; they make him
> heavenly. Men are material; the Manifestations
> transform them into semblance divine. They are
> immature children; the Manifestations develop
> them into maturity. Man is poor; they endow him
> with wealth. Man is base, treacherous and mean;
> the Manifestations of God uplift him into dignity,
> nobility and loftiness. (Abdu'l-Baha, Foundations
> of World Unity, p. 110-111)

Religion teaches that moderation and daily vigilance are
necessary, if we want to be in control of our carnal desires
and corrupt inclinations.

> Such a chaste and holy life, with its implications of
> modesty, purity, temperance, decency and clean-
> mindedness, involves no less than the exercise of
> moderation in all that pertains to dress, language,
> amusements, and all artistic and literary avocations.
> It demands daily vigilance in the control of one's
> carnal desires and corrupt inclinations. (Shoghi
> Effendi, Lights of Guidance, p. 364)

Religion teaches us to protect ourselves and shun anyone who tells you to do anything against the commandments of God, even though they may be quoting from all the right books.

> Therefore, it is incumbent upon all the friends of God to shun any person in whom they perceive the emanation of hatred for the Glorious Beauty of Bahá, though he may quote all the Heavenly Utterances and cling to all the Books." He continues— "Glorious be His Name!—"Protect yourselves with utmost vigilance, lest you be entrapped in the snare of deception and fraud." This is the advice of the Pen of Destiny. ('Abdu'l-Bahá, Star of the West, Vol. 13, No. 1, March 21, pp. 19-25)

Religion teaches us it's important to turn away from satanic promptings, because divine bestowals bring forth unity and agreement, whereas satanic leadings induce hatred and war.

> Therefore, mankind must continue in the state of fellowship and love, emulating the institutions of God and turning away from satanic promptings, for the divine bestowals bring forth unity and agreement, whereas satanic leadings induce hatred and war. (Abdu'l-Baha, The Promulgation of Universal Peace, p. 124)

Religion teaches us we need to use our free will; exert ourselves and make an effort:

> Not only has he to exert himself to acquire spiritual qualities . . . but the development of spiritual qualities is not controlled by nature. Although the

> soul aspires to spiritual things, the acquiring of
> spiritual qualities depends upon effort. It is in this
> domain that man has been given free will. This is
> very similar to a bird which in flight must use its
> wings to counteract the force of gravity. If it fails to
> do this, it will be pulled down instantly by this
> force. (Adib Taherzadeh, The Revelation of
> Bahá'u'lláh v 3, p. 78)

Religion teaches we must be prepared to go through pain;
suffering; tests; deprivation and sacrifice in order to
subdue the self. This is because there is always a reaction
when a force is suppressed.

> In subduing his self with all its manifold aspects,
> he must be prepared to go through pain and
> suffering and tests. This is only natural, for there is
> always a reaction when a force is suppressed.
> Man's material inclinations, when curbed by the
> dictates of his spiritual being, will undergo some
> form of deprivation and sacrifice. (Adib
> Taherzadeh, The Revelation of Bahá'u'lláh v 3, p.
> 78-79)

To be freed from every bond and become attached to the
Kingdom of God, we need to strive to become
characterized with His attributes.

> Strive thine utmost to become godlike,
> characterized with His attributes, illumined and
> merciful, that thou mayest be freed from every
> bond and become attached at heart to the
> Kingdom of the incomparable Lord. This is Bahá'í
> bounty, and this is heavenly light. ('Abdu'l-Bahá,
> Selections from the Writings of 'Abdu'l-Bahá, p.
> 206)

Very few of us have been freed from this darkness and ascended from the world of nature. Those who have been freed, have followed the divine Teachings and served the world of humanity, and, as a result, are resplendent, merciful, illumined and like unto a rose garden:

> Few are those who have been freed from this darkness, who have ascended from the world of nature to the world of man, who have followed the divine Teachings, have served the world of humanity, are resplendent, merciful, illumined and like unto a rose garden. ('Abdu'l-Bahá, Selections from the Writings of 'Abdu'l-Bahá, p. 206)

Benefits to Breaking Free

When we make a sacrifice something of material value in the path of God and wholly for His sake, we are rewarded spiritually. We become detached from the material world and are able to draw closer to God, and thereby fulfil the purpose of our lives.

> In subduing his self with all its manifold aspects, he must be prepared to go through pain and suffering and tests. This is only natural, for there is always a reaction when a force is suppressed. Man's material inclinations, when curbed by the dictates of his spiritual being, will undergo some form of deprivation and sacrifice. For instance, one may sacrifice his comfort and material means in order to help the poor and the needy. In so doing, one is rewarded spiritually, but has to give up something of material value instead. This sacrifice, if carried out in the path of God and for His sake, is most meritorious. It enables the soul to

> become detached from the material world, and
> thus brings it closer to God. This is one of the
> fruits of sacrifice. (Adib Taherzadeh, The
> Revelation of Bahá'u'lláh v 3, p. 78-79)

If we can dominate our lower nature, we can become
detached from this world:

> To the extent that man can dominate his lower
> nature will he become detached from this world.
> (Adib Taherzadeh, The Revelation of Bahá'u'lláh v
> 3, p. 78-79)

WHAT WE KNOW ABOUT OUR HIGHER NATURE

Shifting from the Lower Nature to the Higher

Man is captive of nature and ignorant of the divine world until the breaths of the Holy Spirit lead him out of the physical conditions of limitation and deprivation.

> In the human plane and kingdom man is a captive of nature and ignorant of the divine world until born of the breaths of the Holy Spirit out of physical conditions of limitation and deprivation. Then he beholds the reality of the spiritual realm and Kingdom, realizes the narrow restrictions of the mere human world of existence and becomes conscious of the unlimited and infinite glories of the world of God. ('Abdu'l-Bahá, The Promulgation of Universal Peace, p. 288-289)

Then we get out of our lower natures by letting the flame of God's love burn brightly within our hearts; and feeding that love with His guidance (reading the Writings morning and night). We protect it with our constancy; and guard it with trust and detachment from everything save God; so that the evil whisperings of others won't extinguish its light.

> Deprive not yourselves of the unfading and resplendent Light that shineth within the Lamp of Divine glory. Let the flame of the love of God burn brightly within your radiant hearts. Feed it with the oil of Divine guidance, and protect it within the shelter of your constancy. Guard it within the globe of trust and detachment from all else but God, so that the evil whisperings of the ungodly may not extinguish its light. (Bahá'u'lláh, Gleanings from the Writings of Bahá'u'lláh, p. 325)

We make a conscious choice to pay attention to what's going on around us, and use our powers of discernment, so that if someone tells you something from their lower natures, you put them behind you.

> If anyone comes to you with the book of the wicked, put him behind you. ('Abdu'l-Bahá, Star of the West, Vol. 13, No. 1, March 21, pp. 19-25)

We close our eyes and stop listening to the people of the world and drink from the water of God's knowledge.

> O Kazim, close thine eye to the people of the world; drink the water of knowledge from the heavenly cup bearers, and listen not to the nonsensical utterances of the manifestations of Satan. ('Abdu'l-Bahá, Star of the West, Vol. 13, No. 1, March 21, pp. 19-25)

> Altogether it is evident that man is more noble and superior, that in him there is an ideal power surpassing nature. He has consciousness, volition, memory, intelligent power, divine attributes and virtues of which nature is completely deprived and bereft; therefore, man is higher and nobler by

> reason of the ideal and heavenly force latent and
> manifest in him. (Abdu'l-Baha, The Promulgation
> of Universal Peace, p. 178)

Benefits of living in our Higher Nature

When we live in our higher nature, we are thankful,
desiring to fly only in the high heavens and sing out our
songs to the best of our ability.

> Thankful, the birds of the spirit seek only to fly in
> the high heavens and to sing out their songs with
> wondrous art. ('Abdu'l-Bahá, Selections from the
> Writings of 'Abdu'l-Bahá, p. 175-176)

Helping others

Those of us who understand the dual nature of man have
a responsibility to strengthen; train; assist; nurse; love;
inform and educate others, to restore them to health. This
takes extreme patience; sympathy and love.

> But some souls are weak; we must endeavor to
> strengthen them. Some are ignorant, uninformed
> of the bounties of God; we must strive to make
> them knowing. Some are ailing; we must seek to
> restore them to health. Some are immature as
> children; they must be trained and assisted to
> attain maturity. We nurse the sick in tenderness
> and the kindly spirit of love; we do not despise
> them because they are ill. Therefore, we must
> exercise extreme patience, sympathy and love
> toward all mankind, considering no soul as
> rejected. ('Abdu'l-Bahá, The Promulgation of
> Universal Peace, p. 286-287)

A NEW WAY OF LOOKING AT MYSELF

How many of my beliefs are coming from God's teachings and how many from my own pathways and traditions? I wanted know, so I'm taking the next three weeks to explore that question, through an online course, called "For my Life" – a biblical program based on the teachings of Henry Wright in a book called "A More Excellent Way".

I haven't done much sharing from the heart in this blog before – most of the postings have come from the head and not from the heart. I've lived my life that way for so long, that I'm only just becoming conscious of a desire to change that.

Six short years ago, I described my heart as a huge brick wall – impenetrable. Four years ago, I referred to it as a stone, and was thrilled at the progress I'd made. Now I want to clean out all the debris from my heart; remove the dust and dross; clear out the veils, so that there's room for God to reside in the only place He wants to live, which is in my heart.

So, with a heart open to new ideas and new ways of looking at my life and the world, I had to come face to face with my relationship to God.

My purpose as a Bahá'í is to know God and to worship Him, something I say everyday in the Short Obligatory Prayer. It's become routine, and I frequently say it by rote, so I sometimes need to stop and remind myself of what it means. I often need to ask myself how well I'm living up to my purpose.

Frequently I get caught up in the minutia of living my life, trying to control every aspect in order to feel safe, which is a remnant of years of violence and abuse in the home. I forget that God has chosen me. God is carrying the weight of the world. I don't have to!

I am reminded that God created me because he loves me. He made me in His image. He created me noble. He created me as a "mine rich in gems of inestimable value". This is the truth. Everything else I believe about myself is a lie.

I'm feeling sad as I write this. My heart is breaking for the me that God created, who has been lost for such a long time. O God, help me to get her back. Take my grief and transmute it into certainty and a steadfastness so strong that nothing will ever break it again.

As I Bahá'í, I know I have to love God and love my neighbor, but the abuse I experienced as a child robbed me of my ability to love myself and distanced me from God, because I truly believed I was unlovable. If I truly loved God and my neighbors the way I "love" myself (with hatred, judgment, condemnation), none of us would benefit and it would pull us all down.

I thought it was my right to hate myself. When I started this journey of self-discovery, looking at what happened in my childhood, I truly believed it was my right to hate myself because I was a "worthless piece of s***". Fortunately God sent me an angel in the form of David Sowerby, who asked me ever so gently: "Susan, are you arguing with God?" This helped turn me around. I've come a long way since then, and I have a long way still to go.

God wants me to know the truth so that it can set me free and transform the world. I always thought I was unloveable. I believed it to the core of my being. The abuse taught me that. The actions of my parents and friends and a cruel world taught me that. And I believed it. And it's a lie. I don't want to believe a lie any longer! I need to change my beliefs to match what the Bahá'í Writings say, not the other way round.

My God is the "All-Loving"; the "Ever-Forgiving"; the "All-Compassionate", and not the fearful, wrathful, judgmental god of my parent's teaching.

For most of my life, I've lived as though I truly believed I was unloveable, despite uncontroversial evidence to the contrary. I have lots of well-wishers; lots of people who want to be my friend, and yet, something's always stopped me from being able to feel or receive their love. That has to change, as I recognize I'm defending a position that's indefensible. The only truth that any of us can believe is what we're told in the Bahá'í Writings. Just because I believe something, doesn't make it true – it just makes me sick.

God wants me to accept myself:

> Regard man as a mine rich in gems of inestimable
> value. Education can, alone, cause it to reveal its
> treasures, and enable mankind to benefit
> therefrom. (Bahá'u'lláh, Gleanings from the
> Writings of Bahá'u'lláh, p. 260).

If I substitute my name, I read this quote in a way that's
more personal: Susan, regard yourself as a mine rich in
gems of inestimable value. Education can, alone, cause
you to reveal your treasures, and enable mankind to
benefit therefrom.

Wow!

And He wants me to recognize that there is something
valuable and valued in me. God created me because He
loved me:

> I knew My love for thee; therefore I created thee,
> have engraved on thee Mine image and revealed
> to thee My beauty. (Bahá'u'lláh, Hidden Words,
> Arabic 3).

Susan, I knew My love for you; therefore I created you,
have engraved on you Mine image and revealed to you
My beauty.

And God wants me to see myself as a noble being:

> Noble have I created thee, yet thou hast abased
> thyself. Rise then unto that for which thou wast
> created. (Bahá'u'lláh, Hidden Words Arabic 22).

Noble have I created thee, Susan, yet you have abased yourself. Rise then unto that for which you were created.

Wow again! He's telling me what He wants me to do. Anything less will not benefit mankind! Please God, let that change our interactions! Please God, let me truly believe, in the "twinkling of an eye", with ever fiber of my being, that I am loveable.

We could all try this for ourselves. We all need to read the Bahá'í Writings to find out what God has to say about us and agree with everything He tells us, even though it might go against everything we believe to be true about ourselves. Anything less is disagreeing with the Almighty; we become dis-eased and vulnerable to disease.

So it's time for me pay attention to the idle fancies and vain imaginings arising from my lower nature and listen to God. It's time to open my inner ears so I can examine my thoughts and beliefs, keep the ones that are in line with the Teachings and discard all the others that are veils between me and God. I'm up for the challenge. I'm looking for a new way of being.

A NEW UNDERSTANDING OF MY LOWER NATURE

Shortly after I became a Bahá'í, I learned that I had a lower nature, out of which can develop all the negative qualities seen in man. Truthfully, I didn't give it much thought until this week. What I'm learning in my class has been a real eye opener, as I come to realize that even though I strive to implement all the Bahá'í teachings to the best of my ability, most of my time is spent dwelling in my lower nature. The experiences of abuse I lived through as a child left me with a poor self image, a lot of fear and self-pity, anxiety and depression, none of which are from God. And the best news of all, now that I know about it, I can finally do something about it! Let's take a look at some of the things I'm learning.

We have two selves:

> ... self has really two meanings, or is used in two senses, in the Bahá'í writings; one is self, the identity of the individual created by God. This is the self mentioned in such passages as "he hath known God who hath known himself", etc. The other self is the ego, the dark, animalistic heritage each one of us has, the lower nature that can develop into a monster of selfishness, brutality,

> lust and so on. (Shoghi Effendi, The Compilation
> of Compilations vol II, p. 18)

Our lower nature is sometimes referred to as our ego:

> The ego is the animal in us, the heritage of the
> flesh which is full of selfish desires. (Shoghi
> Effendi, Unfolding Destiny, p. 453)

Our lower natures include our 5 senses (sight, hearing,
taste, touch, smell), by which we receive information from
the world, and sadly, much of it is lies when filtered
through the Bahá'í Writings. I can look at you, hear what
you are saying, and try to filter out if what you are saying
is coming from your higher or lower nature. God's Word
helps us discern truth from falsehood. Here is a process
we've been given for discerning truth from error:

> Consequently, it has become evident that the four
> criteria standards of judgment by which the
> human mind reaches its conclusions (senses,
> intellect, traditional or scriptural and inspiration)
> are faulty and inaccurate. All of them are liable to
> mistake and error in conclusions. But a statement
> presented to the mind, accompanied by proofs
> which the senses can perceive to be correct, which
> the faculty of reason can accept, which is in accord
> with traditional authority and sanctioned by the
> promptings of the heart, can be adjudged and
> relied upon as perfectly correct, for it has been
> proved and tested by all the standards of
> judgment and found to be complete. When we
> apply but one test, there are possibilities of
> mistake. This is self-evident and manifest.

('Abdu'l-Bahá, Promulgation of Universal Peace,
p. 255).

We're caught between our lower and higher natures,
because our lower nature uses the same pathway to speak
to us as God does – through our thoughts. At any given
moment we might be listening to God or to our own idle
fancies. So it's inevitable that we sometimes get confused
about who we are listening to, which is why God asks us
to listen with our inner ear.

Improper thoughts, feelings and emotions are part of our
lower nature. For example, the law of God tells me to
forgive my parents, and my lower nature says that what
they did was unforgiveable. But I know that God's law is
superior to my faulty belief system, because it's the truth.

I'm learning that my mind is renewed by the choices I
make. For example, every time I choose to forgive, I'm
building forgiveness into my soul, and with enough
practice, it becomes a way of life. Every time I don't
choose to forgive, that also builds into my soul and it too
becomes a way of life. So I have to ask myself: which law
do I want to choose?

I may have been trained by my lower nature, but God
gave me free will to rise above it. So again, I ask myself:
Whose voice am I going to listen to?

It's my lower self that I must battle against:

> It is this self we must struggle against . . . in order
> to strengthen and free the spirit within us and

> help it to attain perfection. (Shoghi Effendi, The
> Compilation of Compilations vol II, p. 18-19)

There's a battle going on inside each of us, all the time, but
the battle is not with "ourselves" (both higher and lower).
It's only with our lower nature. The source of conflict
arises when we become one with an evil thought,
believing it to be true. For example, when I was a baby, I
overheard my mother say: "I wish she'd never been born"
and for many years I believed I was unwanted and
unloved. I became one with this belief, and it fed my
desire to die.

We can't serve both "masters" (God and our lower nature)
at the same time. When we try, we become unstable in all
our ways. For example, I can't believe that I am
unloveable and teach that I was created out of God's love
for me. I can't effectively teach the faith while waiting to
die! I'm sure this is the origin of my post traumatic stress
symptoms!

> There'll be no end to longing till I find my heart's
> desire
> Either I'll win my own Heart's Life or lose my life
> entire.
>   (Hafiz, quoted in Marzieh Gail, Dawn
> Over Mount Hira, p. 42)

I'm learning that shame and guilt are caused by believing
the battle is with myself, causing me to hate myself. These
thoughts are coming from my lower nature, and are not
true. Recognizing this, I must cast these negative beliefs
out and cling to what's true:

How well hath it been said; "Cling unto the robe
of the Desire of thy heart, and put thou away all
shame; bid the worldlywise be gone, however
great their name." (Bahá'u'lláh, Kitáb-i-Íqán, pp.
69-70).

Each one of us, if we look into our failures, is sure
to feel unworthy and despondent, and this feeling
only frustrates our constructive efforts and wastes
time. The thing for us to focus on is the glory of
the Cause and the Power of Bahá'u'lláh which can
make of a mere drop a surging sea! (Shoghi
Effendi: Unfolding Destiny, page 447)

What's true is that God loves me, just the way I am:

Out of the wastes of nothingness, with the clay of
My command I made thee to appear, and have
ordained for thy training every atom in existence
and the essence of all created things. Thus, ere
thou didst issue from thy mother's womb, I
destined for thee two founts of gleaming milk,
eyes to watch over thee, and hearts to love thee.
Out of My loving-kindness, 'neath the shade of
My mercy I nurtured thee, and guarded thee by
the essence of My grace and favor. And My
purpose in all this was that thou mightest attain
My everlasting dominion and become worthy of
My invisible bestowals. (Baha'u'llah, The Persian
Hidden Words 29)

Of course, we're all a mixture of both lower and higher
natures. None of us are saints or pure evil. Even when we

try to rid ourselves of one sin, another will crop up.
'Abdu'l-Bahá is reported to have said:

> Just as the earth attracts everything to the centre of
> gravity, and every object thrown upward into
> space will come down, so also material ideas and
> worldly thoughts attract man to the centre of self.
> Anger, passion, ignorance, prejudice, greed, envy,
> covetousness, jealousy and suspicion prevent man
> from ascending to the realms of holiness,
> imprisoning him in the claws of self and the cage
> of egotism.

> The physical man, unassisted by the divine power,
> trying to escape from one of these invisible
> enemies, will unconsciously fall into hands of
> another. No sooner does he attempt to soar
> upward than the density of the love of self, like
> the power of gravity, draws him to the centre of
> the earth. The only power that is capable of
> delivering man from this captivity is the power of
> the Holy Spirit. The attraction of the power of the
> Holy Spirit is so effective that it keeps man ever
> on the path of upward ascension. ('Abdu'l-Bahá,
> Star of the West, Volume 10 - Issue 7)

We are not immune to our lower nature by becoming
Bahá'í. We embark on an active lifestyle as we strive to
"conquer ourselves" and rebuild who we are in God, at
the same time. Like everything, it's a process:

> The House of Justice asks us to point out that the
> recognition of the Manifestation of God is but the
> beginning of a process of growth and that as we

> become more deepened in the Teachings and
> strive to follow His principles, we gradually
> approach more and more the perfect pattern
> which is presented to us. Bahá'u'lláh recognizes
> that human beings are fallible. He knows that, in
> our weakness, we shall repeatedly stumble when
> we try to walk in the path He has pointed out to
> us. (Letters of The Universal House of Justice, 1993
> Jun 05, Homosexuality)

We're all prone to temptation, but God doesn't hold us
responsible for the thoughts that cross our minds; only for
the actions arising from the thoughts. For example when
someone speaks about me with evil, I may be tempted to
repay evil with evil, but that's just temptation. The Bahá'í
Writings teach us how to treat our enemies:

> You must consider your evil-wishers as your well-
> wishers. Those who are not agreeable toward you
> must be regarded as those who are congenial and
> pleasant . . . ('Abdu'l-Bahá, Promulgation of
> Universal Peace, p. 470)

It's not quite as easy as it sounds, though:

> Bahá'u'lláh has clearly said in His Tablets that if
> you have an enemy, consider him not as an
> enemy. Do not simply be long-suffering; nay,
> rather, love him. Your treatment of him should be
> that which is becoming to lovers. Do not even say
> that he is your enemy. Do not see any enemies.
> Though he be your murderer, see no enemy. Look
> upon him with the eye of friendship. Be mindful
> that you do not consider him as an enemy and

> simply tolerate him, for that is but stratagem and hypocrisy. To consider a man your enemy and love him is hypocrisy. This is not becoming of any soul.   (Abdu'l-Baha, The Promulgation of Universal Peace, p. 267)

We can free ourselves from these negative thoughts by submitting ourselves to God, resisting the vain imaginings, and over time, with lots of practice, the thoughts won't hold us captive anymore. Many people try to do this on their own and don't succeed. We can't defeat our lower natures alone. We need to submit to God first, and rise into our higher nature, using a process such as the one described in this quote:

> Through sincere and sustained effort, energized by faith in the validity of the Divine Message, and combined with patience with oneself and the loving support of the Bahá'í community, individuals are able to effect a change in their behaviour; as a consequence of this effort they partake of spiritual benefits which liberate them and which bestow a true happiness beyond description. (Letters of The Universal House of Justice, 1993 Jun 05, Homosexuality).

In order to become doers of God's word, we can ask ourselves:

o   Do my thoughts line up with the teachings of God?
o   Do they line up with the nature of God?
o   Would 'Abdul-Bahá think or act the way I am thinking or want to act?

Sometimes my past gets in the way of separating me from my lower nature, even if I know better. Sometimes I do things contrary to God's will, even when I don't want to, so it was comforting to come across this quote, which might tell me why:

> For once a bird hath grown its wings, it remaineth on the ground no more, but soareth upward into high heaven -- except for those birds that are tied by the leg, or those whose wings are broken, or mired down. (Abdu'l-Baha, Selections from the Writings of Abdu'l-Baha, p. 57)

But now that I'm aware, I can choose differently. I'm coming to see that my lower nature has no blessings to offer – I'm just following a chimera:

> The one who compromises with the law for the sake of his own apparent happiness is seen to have been following a chimera: he does not attain the happiness he sought, he retards his spiritual advance and often brings new problems upon himself. (Universal House of Justice, Lights of Guidance, p. 359)

Living in a materialistic society challenges my ability to separate light from dark. Sometimes my lower nature appears as right, when viewed through the standards current among mankind. For example, one of the ways I coped with the abuse was through perfectionism, workaholism and being driven. These were all qualities valued in the workplace, but they weren't coming from God.

> They follow their own desires and walk in the
> footsteps of the most imperfect and foolish
> amongst them. ('Abdu'l-Bahá, Will & Testament,
> p. 18)

> . . . perfection - which man can never completely
> attain (Shoghi Effendi, The Compilation of
> Compilations vol II, p. 11)

> Regarding the questions you asked in your letter:
> The only people who are truly free of the "dross of
> self" are the Prophets for to be free of one's ego is
> a hallmark of perfection. We humans are never
> going to become perfect, for perfection belongs to
> a realm we are not destined to enter. However, we
> must constantly mount higher, seek to be more
> perfect. (Shoghi Effendi, Unfolding Destiny, p.
> 453)

I'm learning that what I feed grows, and what I neglect,
passes away. The more I meditate on the words of God,
the more it becomes ingrained into me, and becomes who I
am. Rising above my lower nature is one way I can
participate in the process of bringing the Kingdom of God
to earth.

> I adjure Thee by Thy might, O my God! Let no
> harm beset me in times of tests, and in moments of
> heedlessness guide my steps aright through Thine
> inspiration. (The Báb, Baha'i Prayers, p. 28)

When I follow my lower nature, I'm taking direction from
it and making it my God. This causes great anguish in the

Abhá Paradise, as we read in this edited excerpt from the
Tablet of the Holy Mariner:

> Thereupon the countenance of the favored damsel
> beamed above the celestial chambers . . . She
> bestirred herself and perfumed all things in the
> lands of holiness and grandeur.. . When she
> reached that place she rose to her full height in the
> midmost heart of creation . . . And sought to
> inhale their fragrance at a time that knoweth
> neither beginning nor end . . . She found not in
> them that which she did desire . . . She then cried
> aloud, wailed and repaired to her own station
> within her most lofty mansion . . . And raised the
> call amidst the Celestial Concourse and the
> immortal maids of heaven . . . By the Lord! I
> found not from these idle claimants the breeze of
> Faithfulness! . . . She then uttered within herself
> such a cry that the Celestial Concourse did shriek
> and tremble . . . And she fell upon the dust and
> gave up the spirit . . . Thereupon the maids of
> heaven hastened forth from their chambers . . .
> They all gathered around her, and lo! they found
> her body fallen upon the dust . . . And as they
> beheld her state and comprehended a word of the
> tale told by the Youth, they bared their heads, rent
> their garments asunder, beat upon their faces,
> forgot their joy, shed tears and smote with their
> hands upon their cheeks, and this is verily one of
> the mysterious grievous afflictions . . .
> (Bahá'u'lláh, Tablet of the Holy Mariner, Baha'i
> Prayers, p. 225)

Finally, I'm learning it's important to separate the person from the sin. Instead of thinking "there goes an angry person", I'm learning to say: 'there goes a person who has anger".

This isn't just semantics. If anger and rage are removed from a person, what's left? Just the person. This subtle shift allows for compassion. For example, my father had a lot of rage but he wasn't (as I formerly insisted) a rage-aholic. He chose to act in evil ways but he wasn't evil. I can hate what he did to me without hating him. He was only reflecting the evil that was taught to him.

When we recognize we're coming from our lower natures, and sincerely ready to move into a higher plane, we can ask God for forgiveness, using a prayer such as this:

> O God, my God! Have mercy then upon my helpless state, my poverty, my misery, my abasement! Give me to drink from the generous cup of Thy grace and forgiveness, stir me with the sweet scents of Thy love, gladden my bosom with the light of Thy knowledge, purify my soul with the mysteries of Thy oneness, raise me to life with the gentle breeze that cometh from the gardens of Thy mercy -- till I sever myself from all else but Thee, and lay hold of the hem of Thy garment of grandeur, and consign to oblivion all that is not Thee, and be companioned by the sweet breathings that waft during these Thy days, and attain unto faithfulness at Thy Threshold of Holiness, and arise to serve Thy Cause, and to be humble before Thy loved ones, and, in the presence of Thy favoured ones, to be nothingness

itself. Verily art Thou the Helper, the Sustainer,
the Exalted, the Most Generous.   (Abdu'l-
Baha, Selections from the Writings of Abdu'l-Baha,
pp. 4-5)

WE ARE NOT OUR THOUGHTS

The biggest problem about thoughts is this; people don't know the source of their thoughts. They don't stop and ask, "Is that really how God thinks?" or, "Is this thought coming from the kingdom of God or the kingdom of darkness?"

For example: Where did the thought come from, which led Mírzá Yahýá to betray Bahá'u'lláh?

Where did the thought come from, which led Osama Bin Laden to bomb the World Trade Centre?

Where did the thought come from, which led Hitler to want to exterminate the Jews?

These thoughts all came out of their lower natures. Not from God. As "the Omniscient"; "the All-informed" and "the All Knowing", God might have known what was going to happen, but He didn't put the thoughts into their minds. They bought those thoughts as if they were real, and coming from their own minds. Because of their disobedience towards the laws of God, pathways were open for those idle fancies and vain imaginings to take root.

In the course I'm taking this week, I'm reminded that the word of God is the only source of true knowledge. It's the standard by which to judge everything else.

Do you know the source of your own thoughts? Are they coming from God or from your lower nature? The only way to know for sure is to run them through the Bahá'í Writings.

There are 3 sources of thought:

- o   People in the here and now, telling us things

- o   Our lower nature

- o   Our higher nature – or the voice of God

As we know from the passages quoted about the four ways of knowing, we cannot be sure we are hearing the "voice of God" even when striving to listen to our higher nature. For example, my lower nature often tries to trick me by quoting a Writing that I think is coming from my higher nature. I'm inclined to believe it, because it's a quote from the Writings. It would be like a physician prescribing insulin for a patient who needs antibiotics. Both are good when applied at the right time to the right malady; but could be disastrous if applied at the wrong time. It's important to be aware; and to use our powers of discernment.

How do thoughts develop? We're told in the Bahá'í Writings that we see something, which goes into our imagination, then into our thought, comprehension, and memory:

> For instance, sight is one of the outer powers; it
> sees and perceives this flower, and conveys this
> perception to the inner power -- the common
> faculty -- which transmits this perception to the
> power of imagination, which in its turn conceives
> and forms this image and transmits it to the power
> of thought; the power of thought reflects and,
> having grasped the reality, conveys it to the power
> of comprehension; the comprehension, when it
> has comprehended it, delivers the image of the
> object perceived to the memory, and the memory
> keeps it in its repository. (Abdu'l-Baha, Some
> Answered Questions, p. 210-211)

And when we choose to act, our negative thoughts come
from our lower nature. They aren't who we are. I can
think "I'm fat; I'm ugly" or I'm poor, but that isn't who I
am. It's just a thought, and thoughts can be changed.

Negative thoughts come into our minds, flooding us with
feelings and emotions (sounds like a definition of how I
feel when I'm in overwhelm!), as if they were from
ourselves. They distance us from God, resulting in shame
and guilt in a matter of seconds. As a result, we hide from
God, unable to pray, putting us deeper and deeper into
our lower natures. Bahá'u'lláh describes this process so
eloquently:

> Ye are even as the bird which soareth, with the full
> force of its mighty wings and with complete and
> joyous confidence, through the immensity of the
> heavens, until, impelled to satisfy its hunger, it
> turneth longingly to the water and clay of the
> earth below it, and, having been entrapped in the
> mesh of its desire, findeth itself impotent to

> resume its flight to the realms whence it came.
> Powerless to shake off the burden weighing on its
> sullied wings, that bird, hitherto an inmate of the
> heavens, is now forced to seek a dwelling-place
> upon the dust. (Baha'u'llah, Gleanings from the
> Writings of Baha'u'llah, p. 327)

Pride and ego are also manifestations of our lower nature.
For example, perhaps the Kings and Rulers at the time of
Bahá'u'lláh believed that their thoughts were arising from
their own genius, rather than their lower natures, and this
blinded them and caused them to reject the letters
Bahá'u'lláh sent to them.

For many centuries, religious leaders controlled the
thoughts of believers, training them how to think.
Literacy and questions were forbidden. Their
interpretations of scripture was not always based on truth
as set forth in the Words of God, which is why Bahá'u'lláh
abolished the priesthood.

Don't ever believe what a man says, without checking it
out for yourself. Justice demands that we:

> . . . see with thine own eyes and not through the
> eyes of others, and shalt know of thine own
> knowledge and not through the knowledge of thy
> neighbor. (Baha'u'llah, The Arabic Hidden Words
> 2)

We can't stop our lower natures from speaking to us, but
we can choose whether or not we will listen and how we
will respond. In order to do this, we need to hold every
thought captive, so we can discern whose voice we are
listening to.

> Recognizing imperfections, which we all have, is a positive step towards spiritual growth. (The Universal House of Justice, 1993 Jun 05, Homosexuality, p. 6)

And once we've determined whose voice we are listening to, we need to identify the source and cast out all idle fancies and vain imaginings. For example, I'm not usually a person who swears, but whenever I find myself using profanity, I seem unable to rid myself of it, until I can identify the person closest to me who is using those words. Then I stop swearing effortlessly.
Our lower nature trains us how to think:

> The root cause of wrongdoing is ignorance, and we must therefore hold fast to the tools of perception and knowledge. (Abdu'l-Baha, Selections from the Writings of Abdu'l-Baha, p. 136)

What we think and meditate on, becomes a part of who we are.

> The reality of man is his thought . . . (Abdu'l-Bahá, Paris Talks, p. 17)

Henry Wright, in his book "A More Excellent Way", suggests that negative thoughts affect the body, change hormones and neurotransmitters and become habit. We've been given clear guidance on how to reverse this trend:

> I charge you all that each one of you concentrate
> all the thoughts of your heart on love and unity.
> When a thought of war comes, oppose it by a
> stronger thought of peace. A thought of hatred
> must be destroyed by a more powerful thought of
> love. Thoughts of war bring destruction to all
> harmony, well-being, restfulness and content.
> Thoughts of love are constructive of brotherhood,
> peace, friendship, and happiness. (Abdu'l-Baha,
> Paris Talks, p. 29)

If we think evil thoughts long enough, we will become
evil. One way to avoid it, is by using this affirmation,
found in the prayer for spiritual qualities, which starts "O
God, refresh and gladden":

> I will not dwell on the unpleasant things of life.
> (Author Unknown[1], Baha'i Prayers, p. 151)

And education alone can show us how to rise above it:

> Regard man as a mine rich in gems of inestimable
> value. Education can, alone, cause it to reveal its
> treasures, and enable mankind to benefit
> therefrom. (Baha'u'llah, Gleanings from the
> Writings of Baha'u'llah, p. 259)

But true education comes from God:

---

[1] With regard to the status of the prayer, "O God! Refresh and gladden
my spirit" . . . all attempts to locate the original text of the prayer have, so
far, proved unsuccessful. In the absence of the text it is not possible to
authenticate, completely, the prayer in question. (Universal House of
Justice to an individual, 5 June 2006)

> The hope is cherished that ye may obtain true
> education in the shelter of the tree of His tender
> mercies and act in accordance with that which
> God desireth. (Baha'u'llah, Tablets of Baha'u'llah,
> p. 27)

True education is superior to human education in that it:

> releases capacities, develops analytical abilities,
> confidence, will, and goal-setting competencies,
> and instills the vision that will enable them to
> become self-motivating change agents, serving the
> best interests of the community. (Baha'i
> International Community, 1990 Mar 08, Teacher's
> Situation Determining Factor of Quality)

If parents don't educate their children in the ways of God,
they will be called to account for their deeds before a
"stern Lord". This is the only place in the Writings, where
this threat exists!

> It is for this reason that, in this new cycle,
> education and training are recorded in the Book of
> God as obligatory and not voluntary. That is, it is
> enjoined upon the father and mother, as a duty, to
> strive with all effort to train the daughter and the
> son, to nurse them from the breast of knowledge
> and to rear them in the bosom of sciences and arts.
> Should they neglect this matter, they shall be held
> responsible and worthy of reproach in the
> presence of the stern Lord.   (Abdu'l-Baha,
> Selections from the Writings of Abdu'l-Baha, p.
> 126-127)

In order for our thoughts to become aligned with God's thoughts, we need to:

> Immerse yourselves in the ocean of My words, that ye may unravel its secrets, and discover all the pearls of wisdom that lie hid in its depths. (Baha'u'llah, Gleanings from the Writings of Baha'u'llah, p. 136)

In conclusion, we are thinking beings with the power of discernment. We can choose which thoughts to put into our minds. But we can't do this unless we first immerse ourselves in the Ocean of God's words.

As we see from the quotes below, the following are the "minimal daily requirements":

- Reciting the verses of God every morn and eventide

- Deeping in the Writings by day and by night

- Reciting one of the obligatory prayers

- Repeating Alla'u'Abha' ninety five times

> It hath been ordained that every believer in God, the Lord of Judgement, shall, each day, having washed his hands and then face, seat himself and, turning unto God, repeat 'Allah'u'-Abha' ninety-five times. Such was the decree of the Maker of the Heavens when with Majesty and power, He established Himself upon the thrones of His Names. (Bahá'u'lláh: The Kitáb-i-Aqdas, K18, p. 26)

Recite ye the verses of God every morn and eventide. Whoso faileth to recite them hath not been faithful to the Covenant of God and His Testament, and whoso turneth away from these holy verses in this Day is of those who throughout eternity have turned away from God. Fear ye God, O My servants, one and all. (Baha'u'llah, The Kitab-i-Aqdas, p. 73)

The daily obligatory prayers are three in number. The shortest one consists of a single verse which has to be recited once in every twenty-four hours and at midday. The medium (prayer) which begins with the words: 'The Lord is witness that there is none other God but He,' has to be recited three times a day, in the morning, at noon and in the evening. The long prayer which is the most elaborate of the three has to be recited once in every twenty-four hours, and at any time one feels inclined to do so. (Shoghi Effendi, Directives from the Guardian, p. 59)

Now surely, if ever, is the time for us, the chosen ones of Bahá'u'lláh and the bearers of His Message to the world, to endeavor by day and by night, to deepen, first and foremost, the Spirit of His Cause in our own individual lives, and then labor, and labor incessantly to exemplify in all our dealings with our fellow-men that noble Spirit of which His beloved Son 'Abdu'l-Bahá has been all the days of His life a true and unique exponent. ... Shall we not by our daily life vindicate the high claims of His teachings, and prove by our services the influence of His undying Spirit? This surely is our highest privilege,

and our most sacred duty. (Shoghi Effendi, Bahá'í
Administration, p. 35)

BIBLIOGRAPHY

Baha'i Sources (from Ocean)

'Abdu'l-Bahá, Star of the West, Vol. 13.   Chicago: National
Spiritual Assembly of the United States, 1922-1923.

'Abdu'l-Baha. Foundations of World Unity. Wilmette:
Baha'i Publishing Trust, 1968.

'Abdu'l-Baha. Paris Talks. London: Baha'i Publishing
Trust, 1995.

'Abdu'l-Baha. Selections from the Writings of 'Abdu'l-
Bahá. Haifa: Bahá'í World Centre, 1978.

'Abdu'l-Baha. The Promulgation of Universal Peace.
Wilmette: Baha'i Publishing Trust, 1982.

'Abdu'l-Bahá. Tablets of 'Abdu'l-Bahá Abbas. Bahá'í
Publishing Committee, 1909 [2]

'Abdu'l-Baha, Star of the West, v. II. Chicago: National
Spiritual Assembly of the United States, 1911.

'Abdu'l-Baha, Star of the West, vol. VII, Chicago: National
Spiritual Assembly of the United States, 1916.

---

[2] These Tablets have not all been authenticated and many of the
translations are not up to current standards for accuracy.

Baha'u'llah. Gleanings from the Writings of Bahá'u'lláh. Trans. Shoghi Effendi. Wilmette: Baha'i Publishing Trust, 1983.

Bahá'u'lláh. Tablets of Baha'u'llah Revealed After the Kitáb-i-Aqdas. Wilmette: Baha'i Publishing Trust, 1988.

Bahá'u'lláh. The Kitáb-i-Aqdas. Haifa: Bahá'í World Centre, 1992.

Bahá'u'lláh. The Kitáb-i-Iqan. Wilmette: Baha'i Publishing Trust, 1983.

Bahá'u'lláh. The Proclamation of Bahá'u'lláh. Wilmette: Baha'i Publishing Trust, 1978.

Bahá'u'lláh, The Báb, and 'Abdu'l-Bahá. Baha'i Prayers. Wilmette: Baha'i Publishing Trust, 1991.

Bahá'u'lláh. The Hidden Words of Baha'u'llah. Wilmette: Baha'i Publishing Trust, 1975.

Gail, Marzieh. Dawn Over Mount Hira. Oxford: George Ronald, 1976.

Hornby, Helen, comp. and ed. Lights of Guidance: A Baha'i Reference File. New Delhi: Baha'i Publishing Trust, 1994.

Shoghi Effendi, Directives From the Guardian. Wilmette: Bahá'í Publishing Trust, 1973.

Shoghi Effendi, The Unfolding Destiny of the British Bahá'í Community. Oakham: UK Bahá'í Publishing Trust, 1981.

Shoghi Effendi. <u>The Compilation of Compilations,</u> vols I
and II. Maryborough: Bahá'í Publications Australia, 1991.

Taherzadeh, Adib. <u>The Revelation of Bahá'u'lláh v 2</u>.
Oxford: George Ronald, 2006.

Taherzadeh, Adib. <u>The Revelation of Bahá'u'lláh v 3</u>.
Oxford: George Ronald, 1996.

Universal House of Justice. <u>The Universal House of
Justice, Messages 1963 to 1986.</u> Wilmette: Baha'i
Publishing Trust, 1986.

.

ABOUT THE AUTHOR

 Susan Gammage is a Bahá'í-inspired author, educator and researcher with a passion for finding ways to help people apply Bahá'í principles to everyday life situations so they can learn to "live the life". She has published over 600 articles and twelve books and nothing gives her greater pleasure than working on a whole lot more. She is blessed to be able to live in one of the most beautiful parts of Canada.

You can find her on the web at www.susangammage.com

Made in the USA
Monee, IL
12 June 2020